The Pet Tarantula

A True Story

My friend Italo
lives in Laja,
a town in Chile.

Tarantulas live in
the long grass
behind the town.

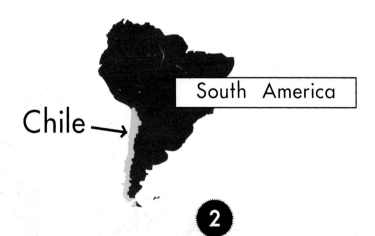

Chile →

South America

3

Italo has caught one
and keeps it as a pet.
He calls it Peluca.
That means furry.

Italo lets Peluca walk
onto his hand.

"Do you want to hold it?"
he asks me.

"Is it poisonous?" I ask.
"Will it bite?"

"Only if you hurt it.
But its bite isn't as bad
as a beesting.
Come on!" Italo says.

Peluca walks onto my hand.
It feels too heavy
to be a spider.

Its body is fat.
It is covered with
soft hairs.

Its legs are hairy, too.
Its feet look like
the ends of my fingers.

"Time for dinner," Italo says.
He puts Peluca back in its box.
He puts some little spiders
in with it.

Peluca bites a spider.
The poison paralyses the spider.
Peluca sucks out the inside
and leaves the skin.

More about Tarantulas

Tarantulas have eight eyes but they cannot see well.

Tarantulas live in many parts of the world.

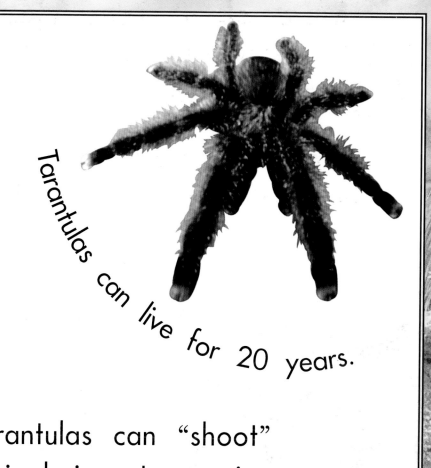

Tarantulas can live for 20 years.

Tarantulas can "shoot"
their hairs at enemies.
Their hairs sting,
and make their enemies itch.

Tarantulas are big enough to eat small birds, mice, and lizards.

Some tarantulas even catch frogs!